50 Italian Soups for Every Season

By: Kelly Johnson

Table of Contents

- Minestrone
- Ribollita
- Zuppa Toscana
- Stracciatella (Italian Egg Drop Soup)
- Pasta e Fagioli
- Pappa al Pomodoro
- Sicilian Cauliflower Soup
- Lentil Soup with Sausage
- Zuppa di Pesce (Fish Soup)
- Tomato Basil Soup
- Cabbage and Potato Soup
- Porcini Mushroom Soup
- Fagioli al Fungo (Beans and Mushroom Soup)
- Chickpea and Spinach Soup
- Carrot and Ginger Soup
- Venetian Pumpkin Soup
- Bean and Kale Soup
- Broccoli and Cheese Soup
- Acquacotta (Tuscan Wild Herb Soup)
- Neapolitan Meatball Soup
- Leek and Potato Soup
- Salsiccia e Fagioli (Sausage and Bean Soup)
- Cabbage and Bean Soup
- Tortellini in Brodo
- Italian Wedding Soup
- Polenta and Mushroom Soup
- Calabrian Chili Soup
- Chicken and Vegetable Minestrone
- Bean and Tomato Soup
- Baked Ziti Soup
- Tuscan Bean Soup with Kale
- Zuppa di Lenticchie (Lentil Soup)
- Pugliese Cabbage Soup
- Sweet Potato and Sausage Soup
- Saffron and Pea Soup

- Creamy Asparagus Soup
- Spicy Tomato and Bread Soup
- Artichoke Soup
- Truffle and Potato Soup
- Pea and Pancetta Soup
- Potato and Leek Soup
- White Bean and Garlic Soup
- Mushroom and Barley Soup
- Fresh Tomato Soup with Basil
- Roasted Red Pepper Soup
- Eggplant and Ricotta Soup
- Fish and Potato Stew
- Italian Sausage and Potato Soup
- Beet and Goat Cheese Soup
- Vegetable Broth with Ricotta Dumplings

Minestrone

Ingredients:

- 2 tbsp olive oil
- 1 onion, chopped
- 2 carrots, diced
- 2 celery stalks, diced
- 2 cloves garlic, minced
- 1 zucchini, diced
- 1 potato, peeled and diced
- 1 cup green beans, cut into 1-inch pieces
- 1 can (14.5 oz) diced tomatoes
- 6 cups vegetable broth
- 1/2 cup pasta (small shells or elbow)
- 1 can (15 oz) cannellini beans, drained and rinsed
- Salt and pepper to taste
- Fresh basil and Parmesan for garnish

Instructions:

1. In a large pot, heat olive oil over medium heat. Add the onion, carrots, celery, and garlic. Cook until softened, about 5 minutes.
2. Add zucchini, potato, green beans, diced tomatoes, vegetable broth, and pasta. Bring to a boil.
3. Reduce heat and simmer for 20-25 minutes, or until the vegetables and pasta are tender.
4. Stir in the cannellini beans and cook for another 5 minutes.
5. Season with salt and pepper, and garnish with fresh basil and grated Parmesan before serving.

Ribollita

Ingredients:

- 2 tbsp olive oil
- 1 onion, chopped
- 2 carrots, diced
- 2 celery stalks, diced
- 4 cloves garlic, minced
- 1 bunch kale, chopped
- 2 cans (15 oz each) cannellini beans, drained and rinsed
- 1 can (14.5 oz) diced tomatoes
- 6 cups vegetable broth
- 4 cups day-old Italian bread, torn into pieces
- Salt and pepper to taste
- Fresh rosemary for garnish

Instructions:

1. In a large pot, heat olive oil over medium heat. Add onion, carrots, celery, and garlic. Cook for 5-7 minutes, until softened.
2. Add kale, cannellini beans, tomatoes, and vegetable broth. Bring to a simmer and cook for 15-20 minutes.
3. Stir in the torn bread pieces and cook for an additional 10 minutes, until the bread softens and the soup thickens.
4. Season with salt and pepper and garnish with fresh rosemary.
5. Serve warm with a drizzle of olive oil.

Zuppa Toscana

Ingredients:

- 2 tbsp olive oil
- 1 lb Italian sausage (spicy or mild)
- 1 onion, chopped
- 3 cloves garlic, minced
- 4 large potatoes, thinly sliced
- 4 cups chicken broth
- 1 bunch kale, chopped
- 1 cup heavy cream
- Salt and pepper to taste
- Red pepper flakes (optional)

Instructions:

1. Heat olive oil in a large pot over medium heat. Add sausage and cook, breaking it up with a spoon, until browned.
2. Add the onion and garlic, cooking for another 5 minutes until softened.
3. Add potatoes and chicken broth, bring to a boil, and simmer for 15-20 minutes, until potatoes are tender.
4. Stir in kale and cook for an additional 5 minutes.
5. Add heavy cream, season with salt and pepper, and red pepper flakes if using.
6. Serve hot, garnished with additional kale if desired.

Stracciatella (Italian Egg Drop Soup)

Ingredients:

- 6 cups chicken broth
- 2 large eggs, beaten
- 1/4 cup grated Parmesan
- 2 tbsp fresh parsley, chopped
- Salt and pepper to taste

Instructions:

1. Bring the chicken broth to a boil in a large pot.
2. In a separate bowl, beat the eggs with Parmesan and a pinch of salt and pepper.
3. Once the broth is boiling, reduce the heat to a simmer. Slowly pour in the egg mixture, stirring constantly to create ribbons of egg.
4. Continue stirring until the eggs are fully cooked.
5. Garnish with fresh parsley and serve immediately.

Pasta e Fagioli

Ingredients:

- 2 tbsp olive oil
- 1 onion, chopped
- 2 carrots, diced
- 2 celery stalks, diced
- 2 cloves garlic, minced
- 1 can (15 oz) cannellini beans, drained and rinsed
- 1 can (15 oz) kidney beans, drained and rinsed
- 6 cups vegetable or chicken broth
- 1 cup small pasta (such as ditalini or elbow macaroni)
- 1 can (14.5 oz) diced tomatoes
- Salt and pepper to taste
- Fresh parsley and Parmesan for garnish

Instructions:

1. Heat olive oil in a large pot over medium heat. Add the onion, carrots, celery, and garlic. Cook until softened, about 5 minutes.
2. Add the cannellini beans, kidney beans, broth, and tomatoes. Bring to a boil.
3. Stir in the pasta and simmer for 10-12 minutes, until the pasta is tender.
4. Season with salt and pepper and garnish with fresh parsley and grated Parmesan before serving.

Pappa al Pomodoro

Ingredients:

- 2 tbsp olive oil
- 1 onion, chopped
- 3 cloves garlic, minced
- 6 ripe tomatoes, chopped
- 4 cups vegetable broth
- 4 cups day-old Italian bread, torn into pieces
- Salt and pepper to taste
- Fresh basil for garnish

Instructions:

1. Heat olive oil in a large pot over medium heat. Add the onion and garlic, cooking until softened.
2. Add the chopped tomatoes and cook for 10 minutes until they break down into a sauce.
3. Pour in the vegetable broth and bring to a simmer.
4. Add the torn bread and stir until the bread absorbs the liquid and the soup thickens.
5. Season with salt and pepper, and garnish with fresh basil before serving.

Sicilian Cauliflower Soup

Ingredients:

- 2 tbsp olive oil
- 1 onion, chopped
- 2 cloves garlic, minced
- 1 medium cauliflower, chopped into florets
- 4 cups vegetable broth
- 1 can (15 oz) cannellini beans, drained and rinsed
- Salt and pepper to taste
- Fresh parsley for garnish

Instructions:

1. Heat olive oil in a large pot over medium heat. Add the onion and garlic, cooking until softened.
2. Add the cauliflower and vegetable broth. Bring to a boil and simmer for 15-20 minutes until the cauliflower is tender.
3. Stir in the cannellini beans and cook for an additional 5 minutes.
4. Season with salt and pepper, and garnish with fresh parsley before serving.

Lentil Soup with Sausage

Ingredients:

- 2 tbsp olive oil
- 1 lb Italian sausage, casing removed
- 1 onion, chopped
- 2 carrots, diced
- 2 celery stalks, diced
- 3 cloves garlic, minced
- 1 cup dried lentils, rinsed
- 6 cups chicken or vegetable broth
- Salt and pepper to taste
- Fresh parsley for garnish

Instructions:

1. Heat olive oil in a large pot over medium heat. Add sausage and cook until browned, breaking it up with a spoon.
2. Add the onion, carrots, celery, and garlic. Cook for 5-7 minutes until softened.
3. Stir in the lentils and broth. Bring to a boil, then reduce heat and simmer for 25-30 minutes, until lentils are tender.
4. Season with salt and pepper and garnish with fresh parsley before serving.

Zuppa di Pesce (Fish Soup)

Ingredients:

- 2 tbsp olive oil
- 1 onion, chopped
- 2 cloves garlic, minced
- 1/2 cup white wine
- 4 cups fish stock
- 1 can (14.5 oz) diced tomatoes
- 1 lb mixed fish fillets (such as cod, haddock, or tilapia), cut into chunks
- 1/2 lb shrimp, peeled and deveined
- 1/2 lb mussels or clams, cleaned
- Salt and pepper to taste
- Fresh parsley for garnish

Instructions:

1. Heat olive oil in a large pot over medium heat. Add the onion and garlic, cooking until softened.
2. Pour in the white wine and cook for 2-3 minutes to reduce slightly.
3. Add fish stock, tomatoes, and bring to a boil. Reduce heat and simmer for 10 minutes.
4. Add the fish fillets, shrimp, and mussels/clams. Cook for an additional 10-12 minutes until the fish is cooked through and the seafood opens.
5. Season with salt and pepper, garnish with fresh parsley, and serve hot.

Tomato Basil Soup

Ingredients:

- 2 tbsp olive oil
- 1 onion, chopped
- 2 cloves garlic, minced
- 6 cups ripe tomatoes, chopped (or 2 cans of diced tomatoes)
- 4 cups vegetable broth
- 1/2 cup fresh basil leaves, chopped
- 1 tsp sugar
- Salt and pepper to taste
- 1/2 cup heavy cream (optional)

Instructions:

1. Heat olive oil in a large pot over medium heat. Add the onion and garlic, and cook until softened, about 5 minutes.
2. Add the chopped tomatoes, vegetable broth, and sugar. Bring to a boil, then reduce the heat and simmer for 20-25 minutes.
3. Use an immersion blender to puree the soup until smooth. Alternatively, blend in batches using a countertop blender.
4. Stir in fresh basil and season with salt and pepper to taste.
5. If desired, add heavy cream to make the soup creamy.
6. Serve hot, garnished with extra basil if desired.

Cabbage and Potato Soup

Ingredients:

- 2 tbsp olive oil
- 1 onion, chopped
- 2 cloves garlic, minced
- 4 cups cabbage, shredded
- 4 large potatoes, peeled and diced
- 6 cups vegetable broth
- Salt and pepper to taste
- Fresh parsley for garnish

Instructions:

1. Heat olive oil in a large pot over medium heat. Add the onion and garlic and cook until softened, about 5 minutes.
2. Add shredded cabbage, potatoes, and vegetable broth. Bring to a boil, then reduce the heat and simmer for 30 minutes, or until potatoes are tender.
3. Season with salt and pepper to taste.
4. Garnish with fresh parsley before serving.

Porcini Mushroom Soup

Ingredients:

- 2 tbsp olive oil
- 1 onion, chopped
- 2 cloves garlic, minced
- 1 cup dried porcini mushrooms, rehydrated and chopped
- 4 cups vegetable broth
- 1 cup heavy cream or milk
- 1 tbsp fresh thyme, chopped
- Salt and pepper to taste
- Fresh parsley for garnish

Instructions:

1. Heat olive oil in a large pot over medium heat. Add the onion and garlic, cooking until softened, about 5 minutes.
2. Stir in the rehydrated porcini mushrooms and cook for 2-3 minutes.
3. Add the vegetable broth and bring to a boil. Reduce the heat and simmer for 15-20 minutes.
4. Stir in the heavy cream or milk and fresh thyme. Continue cooking for another 5 minutes.
5. Use an immersion blender to puree the soup until smooth, or blend in batches using a countertop blender.
6. Season with salt and pepper to taste and garnish with fresh parsley before serving.

Fagioli al Fungo (Beans and Mushroom Soup)

Ingredients:

- 2 tbsp olive oil
- 1 onion, chopped
- 2 cloves garlic, minced
- 2 cups mushrooms, sliced (such as cremini or button mushrooms)
- 1 can (15 oz) cannellini beans, drained and rinsed
- 4 cups vegetable broth
- 1 tsp rosemary, chopped
- Salt and pepper to taste
- Fresh parsley for garnish

Instructions:

1. Heat olive oil in a large pot over medium heat. Add the onion and garlic, and cook until softened, about 5 minutes.
2. Stir in the mushrooms and cook until they release their moisture and begin to brown, about 5-7 minutes.
3. Add the cannellini beans, vegetable broth, and rosemary. Bring to a boil, then reduce the heat and simmer for 20 minutes.
4. Season with salt and pepper to taste.
5. Garnish with fresh parsley before serving.

Chickpea and Spinach Soup

Ingredients:

- 2 tbsp olive oil
- 1 onion, chopped
- 2 cloves garlic, minced
- 1 can (15 oz) chickpeas, drained and rinsed
- 4 cups vegetable broth
- 1/2 tsp cumin
- 1/2 tsp paprika
- 1 bunch spinach, chopped
- Salt and pepper to taste
- Fresh lemon juice for garnish

Instructions:

1. Heat olive oil in a large pot over medium heat. Add the onion and garlic, and cook until softened, about 5 minutes.
2. Stir in the chickpeas, vegetable broth, cumin, and paprika. Bring to a boil, then reduce the heat and simmer for 15-20 minutes.
3. Add the chopped spinach and cook until wilted, about 3-5 minutes.
4. Season with salt and pepper to taste.
5. Garnish with a squeeze of fresh lemon juice before serving.

Carrot and Ginger Soup

Ingredients:

- 2 tbsp olive oil
- 1 onion, chopped
- 2 cloves garlic, minced
- 4 cups carrots, peeled and chopped
- 1-inch piece fresh ginger, peeled and grated
- 4 cups vegetable broth
- Salt and pepper to taste
- Fresh cilantro for garnish

Instructions:

1. Heat olive oil in a large pot over medium heat. Add the onion and garlic, and cook until softened, about 5 minutes.
2. Stir in the carrots and grated ginger, and cook for another 5 minutes.
3. Add the vegetable broth and bring to a boil. Reduce the heat and simmer for 25-30 minutes, or until the carrots are tender.
4. Use an immersion blender to puree the soup until smooth, or blend in batches using a countertop blender.
5. Season with salt and pepper to taste.
6. Garnish with fresh cilantro before serving.

Venetian Pumpkin Soup

Ingredients:

- 2 tbsp olive oil
- 1 onion, chopped
- 2 cloves garlic, minced
- 4 cups pumpkin, peeled and diced
- 4 cups vegetable broth
- 1/2 tsp nutmeg
- 1/2 tsp cinnamon
- Salt and pepper to taste
- Fresh sage for garnish

Instructions:

1. Heat olive oil in a large pot over medium heat. Add the onion and garlic, and cook until softened, about 5 minutes.
2. Stir in the pumpkin and cook for 5 minutes.
3. Add the vegetable broth, nutmeg, cinnamon, and bring to a boil. Reduce the heat and simmer for 20-25 minutes, until the pumpkin is tender.
4. Use an immersion blender to puree the soup until smooth, or blend in batches using a countertop blender.
5. Season with salt and pepper to taste.
6. Garnish with fresh sage before serving.

Bean and Kale Soup

Ingredients:

- 2 tbsp olive oil
- 1 onion, chopped
- 2 cloves garlic, minced
- 1 can (15 oz) white beans (such as cannellini), drained and rinsed
- 4 cups vegetable broth
- 1 bunch kale, chopped
- 1 tsp thyme, chopped
- Salt and pepper to taste
- Fresh lemon juice for garnish

Instructions:

1. Heat olive oil in a large pot over medium heat. Add the onion and garlic, and cook until softened, about 5 minutes.
2. Stir in the white beans, vegetable broth, and thyme. Bring to a boil, then reduce the heat and simmer for 15 minutes.
3. Add the chopped kale and cook for another 10 minutes, until the kale is tender.
4. Season with salt and pepper to taste.
5. Garnish with a squeeze of fresh lemon juice before serving.

Broccoli and Cheese Soup

Ingredients:

- 2 tbsp butter
- 1 onion, chopped
- 2 cloves garlic, minced
- 4 cups broccoli florets
- 4 cups vegetable broth
- 1 cup shredded cheddar cheese
- 1/2 cup heavy cream
- Salt and pepper to taste
- Fresh chives for garnish

Instructions:

1. In a large pot, melt butter over medium heat. Add the onion and garlic, and cook until softened, about 5 minutes.
2. Add the broccoli and vegetable broth. Bring to a boil, then reduce the heat and simmer for 15-20 minutes, until the broccoli is tender.
3. Use an immersion blender to puree the soup until smooth, or blend in batches using a countertop blender.
4. Stir in the shredded cheddar cheese and heavy cream until the cheese is melted and the soup is creamy.
5. Season with salt and pepper to taste.
6. Garnish with fresh chives before serving.

Acquacotta (Tuscan Wild Herb Soup)

Ingredients:

- 3 tbsp olive oil
- 1 onion, chopped
- 2 cloves garlic, minced
- 2 large tomatoes, peeled and chopped
- 1 zucchini, sliced
- 1 bunch wild greens (such as dandelion, nettles, or spinach)
- 6 cups vegetable broth
- 4 slices rustic bread (preferably stale)
- 1/2 cup pecorino cheese, grated
- 2 eggs
- Salt and pepper to taste

Instructions:

1. Heat olive oil in a large pot over medium heat. Add the onion and garlic, and cook until softened, about 5 minutes.
2. Add the tomatoes and zucchini, cooking for another 5 minutes.
3. Stir in the wild greens and vegetable broth. Bring to a boil, then reduce to a simmer for 15-20 minutes.
4. Toast the slices of bread and place them in individual soup bowls.
5. Pour the soup over the bread and crack an egg on top of each serving. Allow the egg to cook in the hot broth for a few minutes.
6. Top with grated pecorino cheese, and season with salt and pepper to taste. Serve immediately.

Neapolitan Meatball Soup

Ingredients:

- 2 tbsp olive oil
- 1 onion, chopped
- 2 cloves garlic, minced
- 1 carrot, chopped
- 1 celery stalk, chopped
- 1 can (14.5 oz) crushed tomatoes
- 6 cups chicken broth
- 1 cup fresh parsley, chopped
- 1/2 cup breadcrumbs
- 1/4 cup grated parmesan cheese
- 1 egg
- Salt and pepper to taste

Instructions:

1. In a bowl, combine breadcrumbs, parmesan cheese, egg, and a pinch of salt and pepper. Mix until the ingredients come together.
2. Form the mixture into small meatballs.
3. Heat olive oil in a large pot over medium heat. Add the onion, garlic, carrot, and celery, and cook until softened, about 5 minutes.
4. Stir in the crushed tomatoes and chicken broth, and bring to a boil.
5. Gently drop the meatballs into the broth and simmer for 20-25 minutes, or until the meatballs are cooked through.
6. Stir in the chopped parsley and season with salt and pepper.
7. Serve hot, garnished with additional parmesan if desired.

Leek and Potato Soup

Ingredients:

- 2 tbsp olive oil
- 2 leeks, cleaned and sliced
- 2 large potatoes, peeled and diced
- 4 cups vegetable broth
- 1 cup heavy cream (optional)
- Salt and pepper to taste
- Fresh chives for garnish

Instructions:

1. Heat olive oil in a large pot over medium heat. Add the leeks and cook until softened, about 5 minutes.
2. Add the diced potatoes and vegetable broth. Bring to a boil, then reduce the heat and simmer for 25 minutes, or until the potatoes are tender.
3. Use an immersion blender to puree the soup until smooth, or blend in batches using a countertop blender.
4. Stir in the heavy cream, if using, and season with salt and pepper to taste.
5. Garnish with fresh chives before serving.

Salsiccia e Fagioli (Sausage and Bean Soup)

Ingredients:

- 2 tbsp olive oil
- 1 lb Italian sausage, casing removed
- 1 onion, chopped
- 2 cloves garlic, minced
- 2 cans (15 oz each) cannellini beans, drained and rinsed
- 4 cups chicken broth
- 1 can (14.5 oz) diced tomatoes
- 1 tsp thyme, chopped
- 1 tsp rosemary, chopped
- Salt and pepper to taste
- Fresh parsley for garnish

Instructions:

1. Heat olive oil in a large pot over medium heat. Add the sausage, breaking it up with a spoon, and cook until browned, about 7-10 minutes.
2. Add the onion and garlic, cooking until softened, about 5 minutes.
3. Stir in the cannellini beans, chicken broth, diced tomatoes, thyme, and rosemary. Bring to a boil, then reduce the heat and simmer for 20 minutes.
4. Season with salt and pepper to taste.
5. Garnish with fresh parsley before serving.

Cabbage and Bean Soup

Ingredients:

- 2 tbsp olive oil
- 1 onion, chopped
- 2 cloves garlic, minced
- 1 small head of cabbage, shredded
- 2 cans (15 oz each) white beans (such as cannellini), drained and rinsed
- 4 cups vegetable broth
- 1 tsp thyme
- Salt and pepper to taste
- Fresh parsley for garnish

Instructions:

1. Heat olive oil in a large pot over medium heat. Add the onion and garlic, cooking until softened, about 5 minutes.
2. Stir in the shredded cabbage and cook for another 5 minutes.
3. Add the white beans, vegetable broth, thyme, and bring to a boil.
4. Reduce the heat and simmer for 20 minutes, or until the cabbage is tender.
5. Season with salt and pepper to taste.
6. Garnish with fresh parsley before serving.

Tortellini in Brodo

Ingredients:

- 6 cups chicken broth
- 1 package (about 9 oz) fresh tortellini
- 1 small onion, chopped
- 1 carrot, chopped
- 1 celery stalk, chopped
- Fresh parsley for garnish
- Grated parmesan cheese (optional)

Instructions:

1. In a large pot, bring the chicken broth to a boil.
2. Add the onion, carrot, and celery, and cook for 10 minutes.
3. Add the fresh tortellini and cook according to the package instructions (about 3-4 minutes).
4. Season with salt and pepper to taste.
5. Serve the soup hot, garnished with fresh parsley and grated parmesan, if desired.

Italian Wedding Soup

Ingredients:

- 2 tbsp olive oil
- 1 onion, chopped
- 2 cloves garlic, minced
- 1/2 cup small pasta (such as acini di pepe)
- 6 cups chicken broth
- 1/2 lb ground beef
- 1/2 lb ground pork
- 1/2 cup breadcrumbs
- 1/4 cup grated parmesan cheese
- 1 egg
- Salt and pepper to taste
- 4 cups fresh spinach, chopped

Instructions:

1. In a bowl, combine the ground beef, ground pork, breadcrumbs, parmesan cheese, egg, salt, and pepper. Form the mixture into small meatballs.
2. Heat olive oil in a large pot over medium heat. Add the onion and garlic, and cook until softened, about 5 minutes.
3. Add the chicken broth and bring to a boil. Drop the meatballs into the broth and cook for 10-12 minutes.
4. Stir in the pasta and spinach, and cook for an additional 5-7 minutes, or until the pasta is tender.
5. Season with salt and pepper to taste, and serve hot.

Polenta and Mushroom Soup

Ingredients:

- 2 tbsp olive oil
- 1 onion, chopped
- 2 cloves garlic, minced
- 4 cups mushrooms, sliced
- 4 cups vegetable broth
- 1 cup polenta
- 1/2 cup heavy cream (optional)
- Salt and pepper to taste
- Fresh parsley for garnish

Instructions:

1. Heat olive oil in a large pot over medium heat. Add the onion and garlic, cooking until softened, about 5 minutes.
2. Stir in the mushrooms and cook until they release their moisture and begin to brown, about 5 minutes.
3. Add the vegetable broth and bring to a boil. Slowly stir in the polenta and reduce the heat to low.
4. Simmer for 15-20 minutes, stirring frequently until the polenta is tender.
5. If desired, stir in the heavy cream to make the soup creamy.
6. Season with salt and pepper to taste.
7. Garnish with fresh parsley before serving.

Calabrian Chili Soup

Ingredients:

- 2 tbsp olive oil
- 1 onion, chopped
- 2 cloves garlic, minced
- 1-2 Calabrian chilies, chopped (or to taste)
- 4 cups chicken broth
- 1 can (14.5 oz) diced tomatoes
- 1 cup white beans, drained and rinsed
- 1/2 cup fresh basil, chopped
- Salt and pepper to taste

Instructions:

1. Heat olive oil in a large pot over medium heat. Add the onion and garlic, cooking until softened, about 5 minutes.
2. Stir in the chopped Calabrian chilies and cook for another 2-3 minutes.
3. Add the chicken broth, diced tomatoes, and white beans, and bring to a boil.
4. Reduce the heat and simmer for 20 minutes.
5. Stir in the fresh basil and season with salt and pepper to taste.
6. Serve hot, garnished with additional basil if desired.

Chicken and Vegetable Minestrone

Ingredients:

- 2 tbsp olive oil
- 1 onion, chopped
- 2 carrots, chopped
- 2 celery stalks, chopped
- 2 cloves garlic, minced
- 2 cups chicken breast, cooked and shredded
- 4 cups chicken broth
- 1 can (15 oz) diced tomatoes
- 1 cup zucchini, chopped
- 1 cup green beans, chopped
- 1 cup small pasta (such as elbow macaroni)
- 1 tsp dried oregano
- Salt and pepper to taste
- Fresh basil for garnish

Instructions:

1. Heat olive oil in a large pot over medium heat. Add the onion, carrots, and celery, and cook until softened, about 5-7 minutes.
2. Stir in the garlic, cooked chicken, chicken broth, and diced tomatoes. Bring to a boil.
3. Add the zucchini, green beans, and pasta. Reduce the heat and simmer for 15-20 minutes until the vegetables and pasta are tender.
4. Season with oregano, salt, and pepper to taste.
5. Serve hot, garnished with fresh basil.

Bean and Tomato Soup

Ingredients:

- 2 tbsp olive oil
- 1 onion, chopped
- 2 cloves garlic, minced
- 1 can (15 oz) white beans, drained and rinsed
- 1 can (14.5 oz) diced tomatoes
- 4 cups vegetable broth
- 1 tsp dried basil
- 1 tsp dried thyme
- Salt and pepper to taste
- Fresh parsley for garnish

Instructions:

1. Heat olive oil in a large pot over medium heat. Add the onion and garlic, cooking until softened, about 5 minutes.
2. Stir in the beans, diced tomatoes, and vegetable broth. Bring to a boil.
3. Add the dried basil, thyme, salt, and pepper. Reduce the heat and simmer for 20 minutes.
4. Use an immersion blender to partially puree the soup, or blend in batches for a smoother texture.
5. Garnish with fresh parsley and serve.

Baked Ziti Soup

Ingredients:

- 2 tbsp olive oil
- 1 onion, chopped
- 2 cloves garlic, minced
- 1 can (15 oz) crushed tomatoes
- 4 cups chicken broth
- 2 cups ziti pasta, uncooked
- 1 tsp dried oregano
- 1/2 tsp red pepper flakes (optional)
- 1 cup ricotta cheese
- 1 cup shredded mozzarella cheese
- Salt and pepper to taste
- Fresh basil for garnish

Instructions:

1. Heat olive oil in a large pot over medium heat. Add the onion and garlic, and cook until softened, about 5 minutes.
2. Stir in the crushed tomatoes and chicken broth. Bring to a boil.
3. Add the ziti pasta, oregano, red pepper flakes, salt, and pepper. Reduce the heat and simmer for 10-12 minutes until the pasta is tender.
4. Stir in the ricotta and mozzarella cheese, cooking until melted and creamy.
5. Garnish with fresh basil and serve.

Tuscan Bean Soup with Kale

Ingredients:

- 2 tbsp olive oil
- 1 onion, chopped
- 2 cloves garlic, minced
- 2 carrots, chopped
- 2 celery stalks, chopped
- 1 can (15 oz) white beans, drained and rinsed
- 4 cups vegetable broth
- 2 cups kale, chopped
- 1 tsp dried rosemary
- Salt and pepper to taste
- Fresh Parmesan cheese for garnish

Instructions:

1. Heat olive oil in a large pot over medium heat. Add the onion, garlic, carrots, and celery, and cook until softened, about 5 minutes.
2. Stir in the white beans, vegetable broth, kale, and rosemary. Bring to a boil.
3. Reduce the heat and simmer for 20 minutes until the vegetables are tender.
4. Season with salt and pepper to taste.
5. Serve hot, garnished with fresh Parmesan cheese.

Zuppa di Lenticchie (Lentil Soup)

Ingredients:

- 2 tbsp olive oil
- 1 onion, chopped
- 2 cloves garlic, minced
- 2 carrots, chopped
- 2 celery stalks, chopped
- 1 cup dried lentils, rinsed
- 1 can (14.5 oz) diced tomatoes
- 4 cups vegetable broth
- 1 tsp cumin
- 1 tsp dried thyme
- Salt and pepper to taste
- Fresh parsley for garnish

Instructions:

1. Heat olive oil in a large pot over medium heat. Add the onion, garlic, carrots, and celery, and cook until softened, about 5-7 minutes.
2. Stir in the lentils, diced tomatoes, vegetable broth, cumin, thyme, salt, and pepper. Bring to a boil.
3. Reduce the heat and simmer for 30-35 minutes, until the lentils are tender.
4. Garnish with fresh parsley before serving.

Pugliese Cabbage Soup

Ingredients:

- 2 tbsp olive oil
- 1 onion, chopped
- 2 cloves garlic, minced
- 1 small head of cabbage, shredded
- 2 potatoes, peeled and diced
- 4 cups vegetable broth
- 1 can (15 oz) cannellini beans, drained and rinsed
- 1/2 tsp dried thyme
- Salt and pepper to taste

Instructions:

1. Heat olive oil in a large pot over medium heat. Add the onion and garlic, and cook until softened, about 5 minutes.
2. Stir in the cabbage, potatoes, vegetable broth, cannellini beans, thyme, salt, and pepper. Bring to a boil.
3. Reduce the heat and simmer for 25 minutes, or until the potatoes are tender.
4. Season with additional salt and pepper if needed.
5. Serve hot.

Sweet Potato and Sausage Soup

Ingredients:

- 2 tbsp olive oil
- 1 lb Italian sausage, casing removed
- 1 onion, chopped
- 2 cloves garlic, minced
- 2 large sweet potatoes, peeled and diced
- 4 cups chicken broth
- 1 can (14.5 oz) diced tomatoes
- 1 tsp smoked paprika
- 1 tsp thyme
- Salt and pepper to taste
- Fresh parsley for garnish

Instructions:

1. Heat olive oil in a large pot over medium heat. Add the sausage, breaking it up with a spoon, and cook until browned.
2. Add the onion and garlic, and cook until softened, about 5 minutes.
3. Stir in the sweet potatoes, chicken broth, diced tomatoes, smoked paprika, and thyme. Bring to a boil.
4. Reduce the heat and simmer for 20-25 minutes, until the sweet potatoes are tender.
5. Season with salt and pepper to taste.
6. Garnish with fresh parsley before serving.

Saffron and Pea Soup

Ingredients:

- 2 tbsp olive oil
- 1 onion, chopped
- 2 cloves garlic, minced
- 1 tsp saffron threads
- 4 cups vegetable broth
- 2 cups frozen peas
- 1/2 cup heavy cream
- Salt and pepper to taste

Instructions:

1. Heat olive oil in a large pot over medium heat. Add the onion and garlic, and cook until softened, about 5 minutes.
2. Stir in the saffron threads and vegetable broth. Bring to a boil.
3. Add the frozen peas and cook for 5-7 minutes until tender.
4. Use an immersion blender to puree the soup until smooth, or blend in batches.
5. Stir in the heavy cream, and season with salt and pepper to taste.
6. Serve hot.

Creamy Asparagus Soup

Ingredients:

- 2 tbsp olive oil
- 1 onion, chopped
- 2 cloves garlic, minced
- 1 bunch asparagus, trimmed and chopped
- 4 cups vegetable broth
- 1/2 cup heavy cream
- Salt and pepper to taste

Instructions:

1. Heat olive oil in a large pot over medium heat. Add the onion and garlic, cooking until softened, about 5 minutes.
2. Stir in the asparagus and cook for another 5 minutes.
3. Add the vegetable broth and bring to a boil. Simmer for 10 minutes until the asparagus is tender.
4. Use an immersion blender to puree the soup until smooth, or blend in batches.
5. Stir in the heavy cream and season with salt and pepper to taste.
6. Serve hot.

Spicy Tomato and Bread Soup

Ingredients:

- 2 tbsp olive oil
- 1 onion, chopped
- 2 cloves garlic, minced
- 1 can (15 oz) diced tomatoes
- 4 cups vegetable broth
- 1/2 tsp red pepper flakes
- 4 slices stale bread, torn into pieces
- Salt and pepper to taste
- Fresh basil for garnish

Instructions:

1. Heat olive oil in a large pot over medium heat. Add the onion and garlic, and cook until softened, about 5 minutes.
2. Stir in the diced tomatoes, vegetable broth, red pepper flakes, and bread. Bring to a boil.
3. Reduce the heat and simmer for 10-15 minutes until the bread breaks down and thickens the soup.
4. Season with salt and pepper to taste.
5. Serve hot, garnished with fresh basil.

Artichoke Soup

Ingredients:

- 2 tbsp olive oil
- 1 onion, chopped
- 2 cloves garlic, minced
- 4 cups artichoke hearts (fresh or frozen), chopped
- 4 cups vegetable broth
- 1/2 cup white wine
- 1 tsp lemon juice
- Salt and pepper to taste
- Fresh parsley for garnish

Instructions:

1. Heat olive oil in a large pot over medium heat. Add the onion and garlic, cooking until softened, about 5 minutes.
2. Stir in the artichoke hearts and cook for another 5 minutes.
3. Add the vegetable broth, white wine, and lemon juice. Bring to a boil.
4. Reduce the heat and simmer for 20 minutes until the artichokes are tender.
5. Use an immersion blender to puree the soup until smooth, or blend in batches.
6. Season with salt and pepper to taste and serve hot, garnished with fresh parsley.

Truffle and Potato Soup

Ingredients:

- 2 tbsp olive oil
- 1 onion, chopped
- 2 cloves garlic, minced
- 4 large potatoes, peeled and diced
- 4 cups vegetable broth
- 1 tbsp truffle oil
- 1/2 cup heavy cream
- Salt and pepper to taste
- Fresh chives for garnish

Instructions:

1. Heat olive oil in a large pot over medium heat. Add the onion and garlic, and cook until softened, about 5 minutes.
2. Stir in the potatoes and vegetable broth. Bring to a boil.
3. Reduce the heat and simmer for 20 minutes, until the potatoes are tender.
4. Use an immersion blender to puree the soup until smooth, or blend in batches.
5. Stir in the truffle oil and heavy cream. Season with salt and pepper to taste.
6. Serve hot, garnished with fresh chives.

Pea and Pancetta Soup

Ingredients:

- 2 tbsp olive oil
- 1 onion, chopped
- 2 cloves garlic, minced
- 1 cup pancetta, diced
- 4 cups vegetable broth
- 4 cups frozen peas
- 1/2 tsp dried mint
- Salt and pepper to taste
- Fresh mint leaves for garnish

Instructions:

1. Heat olive oil in a large pot over medium heat. Add the onion and garlic, cooking until softened, about 5 minutes.
2. Stir in the pancetta and cook until crispy, about 5 minutes.
3. Add the vegetable broth and peas, and bring to a boil.
4. Reduce the heat and simmer for 10-15 minutes, until the peas are tender.
5. Use an immersion blender to puree the soup until smooth, or blend in batches.
6. Stir in the dried mint and season with salt and pepper to taste.
7. Serve hot, garnished with fresh mint leaves.

Potato and Leek Soup

Ingredients:

- 2 tbsp olive oil
- 2 leeks, cleaned and sliced
- 2 cloves garlic, minced
- 4 large potatoes, peeled and diced
- 4 cups vegetable broth
- 1 cup heavy cream
- Salt and pepper to taste
- Fresh chives for garnish

Instructions:

1. Heat olive oil in a large pot over medium heat. Add the leeks and garlic, cooking until softened, about 5 minutes.
2. Add the potatoes and vegetable broth. Bring to a boil.
3. Reduce the heat and simmer for 20 minutes, until the potatoes are tender.
4. Use an immersion blender to puree the soup until smooth, or blend in batches.
5. Stir in the heavy cream and season with salt and pepper to taste.
6. Serve hot, garnished with fresh chives.

White Bean and Garlic Soup

Ingredients:

- 2 tbsp olive oil
- 1 onion, chopped
- 6 cloves garlic, minced
- 2 cans (15 oz each) white beans, drained and rinsed
- 4 cups vegetable broth
- 1 tsp dried rosemary
- Salt and pepper to taste
- Fresh parsley for garnish

Instructions:

1. Heat olive oil in a large pot over medium heat. Add the onion and garlic, cooking until softened, about 5 minutes.
2. Stir in the white beans, vegetable broth, and dried rosemary. Bring to a boil.
3. Reduce the heat and simmer for 20 minutes.
4. Use an immersion blender to puree the soup until smooth, or blend in batches.
5. Season with salt and pepper to taste and serve hot, garnished with fresh parsley.

Mushroom and Barley Soup

Ingredients:

- 2 tbsp olive oil
- 1 onion, chopped
- 2 cloves garlic, minced
- 2 cups mushrooms, sliced
- 1 cup barley
- 4 cups vegetable broth
- 1 tsp dried thyme
- Salt and pepper to taste
- Fresh parsley for garnish

Instructions:

1. Heat olive oil in a large pot over medium heat. Add the onion and garlic, cooking until softened, about 5 minutes.
2. Stir in the mushrooms and cook until tender, about 5 minutes.
3. Add the barley, vegetable broth, and dried thyme. Bring to a boil.
4. Reduce the heat and simmer for 30-40 minutes, until the barley is tender.
5. Season with salt and pepper to taste and serve hot, garnished with fresh parsley.

Fresh Tomato Soup with Basil

Ingredients:

- 6 cups ripe tomatoes, chopped
- 1 medium onion, chopped
- 2 cloves garlic, minced
- 1 tbsp olive oil
- 2 cups vegetable broth
- 1/4 cup fresh basil leaves, chopped
- Salt and pepper to taste
- Fresh basil for garnish

Instructions:

1. Heat olive oil in a large pot over medium heat. Add the onion and garlic, cooking until softened, about 5 minutes.
2. Stir in the chopped tomatoes and cook for 10 minutes, until they release their juices.
3. Add the vegetable broth and bring to a boil. Reduce the heat and simmer for 20 minutes.
4. Use an immersion blender to puree the soup until smooth, or blend in batches.
5. Stir in the fresh basil and season with salt and pepper to taste.
6. Serve hot, garnished with fresh basil.

Roasted Red Pepper Soup

Ingredients:

- 4 large red bell peppers, roasted and peeled
- 1 medium onion, chopped
- 2 cloves garlic, minced
- 2 cups vegetable broth
- 1 tbsp olive oil
- 1/2 tsp smoked paprika
- Salt and pepper to taste
- Fresh cream for garnish (optional)

Instructions:

1. Roast the bell peppers by placing them under the broiler or on a grill until charred. Peel off the skin and remove the seeds.
2. Heat olive oil in a pot over medium heat. Add the onion and garlic, cooking until softened, about 5 minutes.
3. Add the roasted red peppers and vegetable broth to the pot. Stir in the smoked paprika.
4. Bring to a boil, then reduce the heat and simmer for 10 minutes.
5. Use an immersion blender to puree the soup until smooth, or blend in batches.
6. Season with salt and pepper to taste. Serve hot, with a drizzle of fresh cream if desired.

Eggplant and Ricotta Soup

Ingredients:

- 2 medium eggplants, peeled and diced
- 1 medium onion, chopped
- 2 cloves garlic, minced
- 1 cup ricotta cheese
- 4 cups vegetable broth
- 1 tbsp olive oil
- Salt and pepper to taste
- Fresh basil for garnish

Instructions:

1. Heat olive oil in a large pot over medium heat. Add the onion and garlic, cooking until softened, about 5 minutes.
2. Add the diced eggplant and cook for another 10 minutes, stirring occasionally.
3. Add the vegetable broth and bring to a boil. Reduce the heat and simmer for 20 minutes.
4. Use an immersion blender to puree the soup until smooth.
5. Stir in the ricotta cheese and season with salt and pepper to taste.
6. Serve hot, garnished with fresh basil.

Fish and Potato Stew

Ingredients:

- 1 lb white fish fillets (such as cod or haddock), cut into chunks
- 2 medium potatoes, peeled and diced
- 1 medium onion, chopped
- 2 cloves garlic, minced
- 4 cups fish stock or vegetable broth
- 1 tbsp olive oil
- 1 tsp dried thyme
- Salt and pepper to taste
- Fresh parsley for garnish

Instructions:

1. Heat olive oil in a large pot over medium heat. Add the onion and garlic, cooking until softened, about 5 minutes.
2. Add the diced potatoes and cook for another 5 minutes.
3. Pour in the fish stock or vegetable broth and bring to a boil. Reduce the heat and simmer for 15 minutes, or until the potatoes are tender.
4. Add the fish fillets, thyme, salt, and pepper. Cook for 5-7 minutes, until the fish is cooked through.
5. Serve hot, garnished with fresh parsley.

Italian Sausage and Potato Soup

Ingredients:

- 1 lb Italian sausage, crumbled
- 4 medium potatoes, peeled and diced
- 1 medium onion, chopped
- 2 cloves garlic, minced
- 4 cups chicken broth
- 1/2 tsp dried rosemary
- 1/2 cup heavy cream
- Salt and pepper to taste
- Fresh parsley for garnish

Instructions:

1. In a large pot, cook the crumbled sausage over medium heat until browned. Remove excess fat.
2. Add the onion and garlic, cooking until softened, about 5 minutes.
3. Add the diced potatoes, chicken broth, and rosemary. Bring to a boil.
4. Reduce the heat and simmer for 20 minutes, until the potatoes are tender.
5. Stir in the heavy cream and season with salt and pepper to taste.
6. Serve hot, garnished with fresh parsley.

Beet and Goat Cheese Soup

Ingredients:

- 4 medium beets, peeled and diced
- 1 medium onion, chopped
- 2 cloves garlic, minced
- 4 cups vegetable broth
- 1 tbsp olive oil
- 1/2 cup crumbled goat cheese
- Salt and pepper to taste
- Fresh dill for garnish

Instructions:

1. Heat olive oil in a large pot over medium heat. Add the onion and garlic, cooking until softened, about 5 minutes.
2. Add the diced beets and cook for 10 minutes.
3. Pour in the vegetable broth and bring to a boil. Reduce the heat and simmer for 30 minutes, until the beets are tender.
4. Use an immersion blender to puree the soup until smooth.
5. Stir in the goat cheese and season with salt and pepper to taste.
6. Serve hot, garnished with fresh dill.

Vegetable Broth with Ricotta Dumplings

Ingredients for Broth:

- 6 cups vegetable broth
- 1 medium onion, chopped
- 2 carrots, peeled and chopped
- 2 celery stalks, chopped
- 2 cloves garlic, minced
- Salt and pepper to taste

Ingredients for Ricotta Dumplings:

- 1 cup ricotta cheese
- 1/2 cup flour
- 1 egg
- 1/4 cup grated Parmesan cheese
- Salt and pepper to taste

Instructions:

1. For the broth, heat the vegetable broth in a large pot over medium heat. Add the onion, carrots, celery, garlic, salt, and pepper. Bring to a boil.
2. Reduce the heat and simmer for 30 minutes.
3. For the dumplings, mix the ricotta cheese, flour, egg, Parmesan, salt, and pepper in a bowl until smooth.
4. Using a spoon, form small dumplings and drop them into the simmering broth.
5. Continue to cook for 10 minutes, until the dumplings float and are cooked through.
6. Serve the vegetable broth with the ricotta dumplings hot.

www.ingramcontent.com/pod-product-compliance
Lightning Source LLC
LaVergne TN
LVHW081340060526
838201LV00055B/2755